THE ANTI COLOURING BOOK

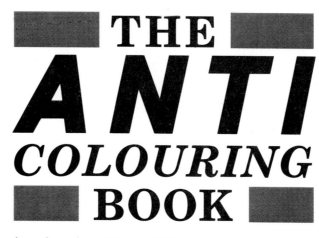

The colouring book with a difference. No dreary pictures to fill in with your felt-tipped pen, but a collection of ideas that will make your fingers itch to get started. Who could resist the chance to draw the worst nightmare you ever had, or your own mug shot and fingerprints, and your idea of what God looks like? Let your imagination run riot with your own newspaper picture of the Martians landing, and your design for a wrapper and name for a new chocolate bar.

Every idea has its own beautifully drawn frame, and some pictures are partially drawn to complete as you will. The Anti-Colouring Book is irresistible.

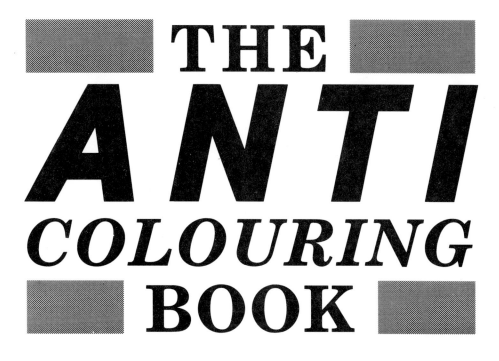

THE ANTI COLOURING BOOK

Hippo Books
Scholastic Children's Books
London

To Michael J. Striker
Stephen, Howard, and Rachel Kimmel

Special thanks for their help and inspiration to
Herbeta W. Sinkus, Herb Perr, John Striker, Joan Imbrogno,
and to all our students, especially John Mengel, Philip Popielarski,
and Peter Popielarski.

*"If we pretend to respect the artist at all.
we must allow . . . freedom of choice. . . .
Art derives a considerable part of its beneficial
exercise from flying in the face of presumptions."*
Henry James

Scholastic Children's Books,
Scholastic Publications Ltd,
7-9 Pratt Street, London NW1 0AE, UK

Scholastic Inc.,
730 Broadway, New York, NY 10003, USA

Scholastic Canada Ltd,
123 Newkirk Road, Richmond Hill,
Ontario, Canada L4C 3G5

Ashton Scholastic Pty Ltd,
P O Box 579, Gosford, New South Wales,
Australia

Ashton Scholastic Ltd,
Private Bag 1, Penrose, Auckland,
New Zealand

First published in the USA by Holt, Rinehart and
Winston 1978

First published by Scholastic Publications Ltd, 1979
Copyright © 1978 by Susan Striker and Edward Kimmel

20 19 18 17 16 15 14 13 12 11

Printed in Finland by
Algraphics Oy/Tampereen Arpatehdas

Grateful acknowledgment is made to Dr.
Irene Russell and the National Art Education
Association for permission to use drawings
from *Research Bulletin*, Vol. 3, No. 1. 1952,
and to Michele Irvin for permission to
reproduce her photograph.

Introduction

PICASSO ONCE SAID THAT he wished he could draw as well as a child. This book is intended to set free the child in all of us. Every project is designed to stimulate the imagination and spark creativity, to generate fantasy and expand a child's frame of reference. Most important, there is no uniform solution or correct answer to any of these projects. They encourage flexibility of thinking and fluency of ideas, and it is unlikely that any two individuals will complete a drawing the same way. A child's finished drawing will be intensely personal and highly individual, and, we hope, will represent his or her emotions, intellectual capabilities, physical development, perceptual awareness, interests, and aesthetic tastes.

The artistic impulse is universal. Jackson Pollock said, "Art is a state of being. An artist paints what he [or she] is." Painting something that comes from within fulfils a genuine need. The child who never discovers art as an outlet must seek other forms of expression. The closest many urban youngsters have come to expressing themselves with paint recently has been to spray their names on walls.

For too many children, "art" experiences have been reduced to such passive activities as painting by numbers, colouring, tracing, and "string art." None of these activities approaches the real meaning of art for children: self-expression. Although we have placed our children in front of television sets and offered them only the most passive art experiences, we have not been able to stifle their basic need to express themselves. We must direct that need by providing children with opportunities to participate actively and self-confidently in art activities that stimulate and excite them.

Children who are not given paper will draw on walls or in the sand. At about the age of two, children spontaneously begin to scribble. After a while, they give names to their scribbles and later tell long stories about what these scribbles represent. Young children derive tremendous joy and satisfaction from their art.

Unfortunately, most adults judge a child's drawing by how accurately it depicts reality. They overlook the most significant aspect of early scribblings, the fact that these drawings represent an important stage of artistic development, as well as provide for imaginative thinking. While parents expect their children to crawl before they walk, they don't always see the importance of the various steps of creative activity necessary for all children to develop inventive minds and the ability to think for themselves.

However, we make the mistake of trying to convince children that their drawings must look a certain way in order to be acceptable. We give them colouring books that consist of drawings by highly skilled professional artists; we ask them to abandon their own adventurous journey toward creativity and stay within the lines. By the time they have completed the first few pages of the average colouring book, the only thing they will have learned is that adults draw better, by adult standards, than they do. At this point most children spurn their own refreshing and expressive drawings.

Dr. Irene Russell's classic example is typical of the proof research has uncovered that the imitative procedures found in colouring books rob children of their abilities to think independently and to express their feelings through art. The first drawing (a) shows a child's depiction of a bird before the child was exposed to colouring books. Once asked to copy a colouring book illustration (b), the child lost originality in subsequent drawings of birds (c).

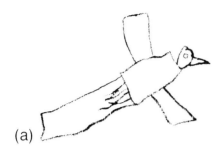

(a)

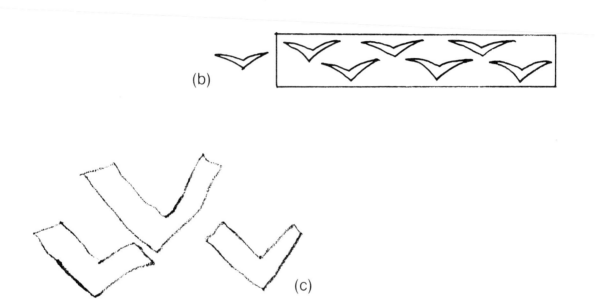

(b)

(c)

How accurate a picture looks when completed is of no consequence to a child. The satisfaction comes from the experience of drawing and painting itself. The joy is in actively participating in the art experience.

This book was not written for those rare but fortunate children whose art remains untouched by adult interference. Such children need only blank pieces of paper and their own deeply rooted creative impulses. This book is for anyone who has ever said "I can't draw" or "I don't know what to draw." It is, in effect, an anti-colouring book, designed to help counteract the many other books that promote anti-child activities. We hope to rekindle the excitement of fantasy, to reawaken the senses, and to reaffirm individuality and self-expression. We hope, too, that many adults will rediscover the sense of freedom and adventure that art can give them. Leave your inhibitions behind, and have fun.

You are a space pioneer. Design a flag for your new planet.

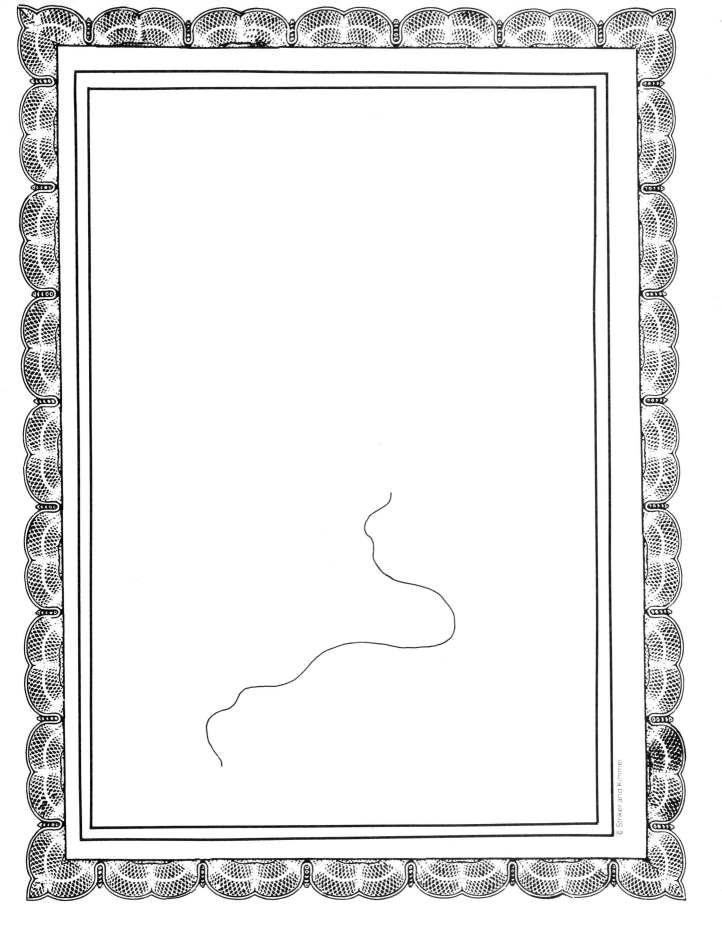

A famous artist needs your help. The artist started
this picture but was stung on the thumb by a bee.
Turn the picture any way you'd like and finish it.

FIRST DAY OF ISSUE

A.

arth

Design a postage stamp for the first
letter mailed from Mars.

Name of fish: _____

Discovered by: _____

Place discovered: _____

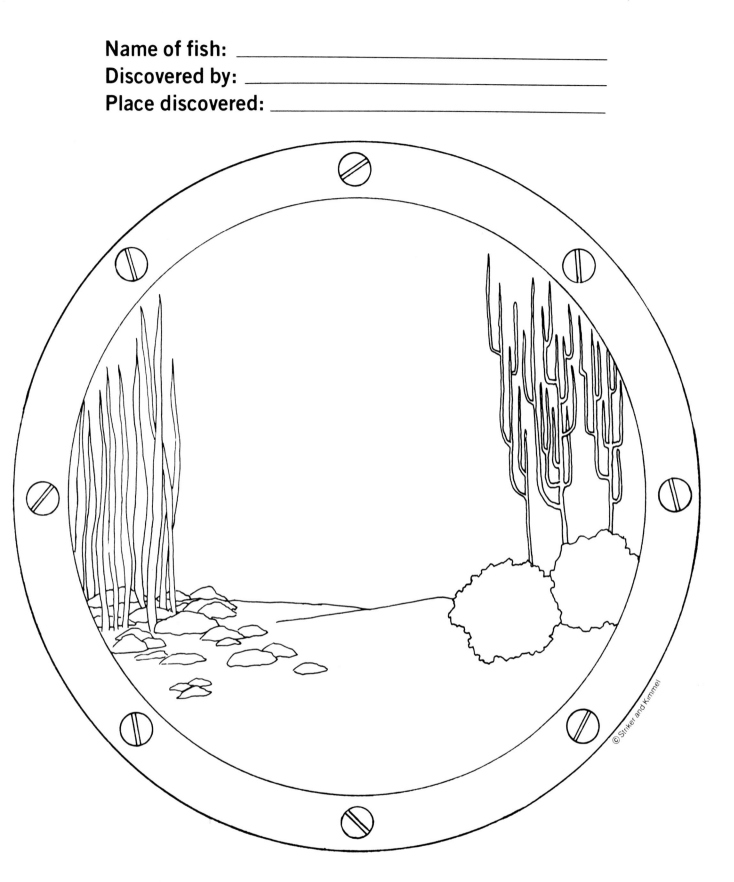

Scientists have just found a new species of fish, but they haven't named it yet. What do you think it looks like and what would you call it?

What was the nicest dream you ever had?

Draw the worst nightmare you ever had.

25¢ DAILY

Vol. 1 No. 1   I hy oho II I - lo ucynollo du cyul u> ulu i ldi/ oho II

EXTRA! EXTRA!
MARTIANS LAND

FUNCTION: _____
_____

DESIGN A ROBOT
THAT WILL DO A CHORE
YOU DON'T LIKE DOING

What would you do with a fortune?

Felix

Design a shopping bag for the fanciest store in the world.

What is the photographer taking a picture of?

This clown has learned how to become invisible. We can
see only this circle. What part of the clown do you think the circle is?

Can you change this pair of scissors into
something completely different? Turn the
paper any way you want to.

Design a family crest that tells something about you and your family.

WANTED

FOR: £5,000,009

©Striker and Kimmel

NAME: FIONA **ALIAS:** FIFI

Fingerprints

Did you ever think about doing something terrible? Pretend that you did it.
Describe the crime you committed, and make your own mug shot and fingerprints.

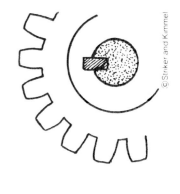

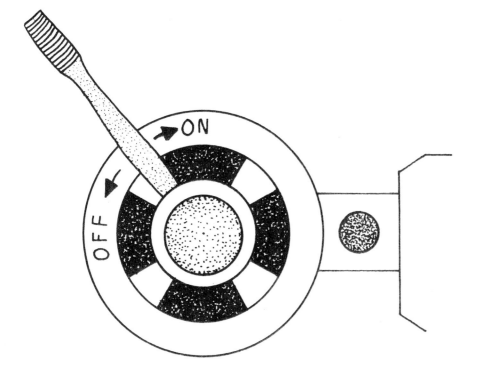

You have just invented a machine that will change the lives of everyone on earth. Only you understand the invention well enough to complete the picture.

What would you add to each scene to show the changes in the four seasons?

© Striker and Kimmel

Do you see your future in this crystal ball?

TO: FROM:

Today is your birthday. Inside this box is the
present you want most in the world. Can you see it?

FLOWER SOCIETY

Name of flower: _____
_____
_____

Discovered by: _____
_____
_____

Place discovered: _____
_____
_____

What does it smell like? _____
_____
_____

How do you know that it is poisonous? _____
_____
_____

Size of blossom: _____
_____
_____

Any other information: _____
_____
_____
_____
_____
_____
_____
_____
_____
_____
_____
_____
_____
_____
_____

You have discovered a poisonous flower growing in your garden. Scientists have asked you to draw a picture of it, name it, and tell something about how you found it.

**What are these people
looking at?**

Where in the world would you like to go to see
a rainbow?

A group of explorers found a rare bird deep in the jungle. They sent back this drawing of the bird sitting in a tree.

Do you ever lie on your back and imagine that you see pictures in the clouds? What do you see in these clouds?

The Daily Paper

20¢   *Vol. 12 No. 24*   **August 25, 1987**

HERO!

You have just performed a heroic deed.
This is the picture and story in the newspaper the next day.

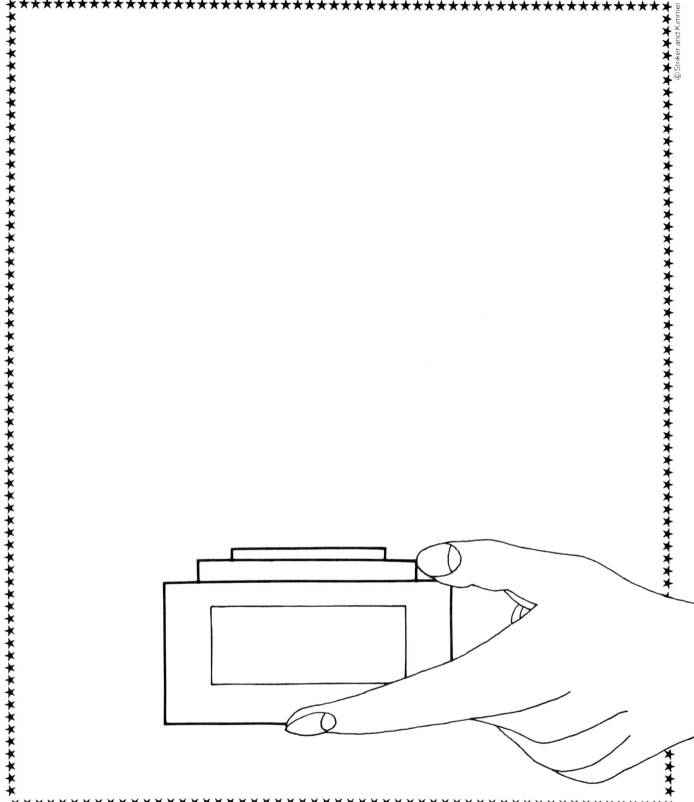

To whom would you give a trophy and what would it look like?

This man is thinking about how he ended up in jail.

Half of this photograph is missing. Can you complete it?

Some people think there is a man or a woman in the moon, and others say the moon is made of green cheese. What do you think of when you look at the moon?

GOD

WHAT DO YOU THINK
GOD LOOKS LIKE?

_____ ,

_____
_____
_____
_____
_____
_____
_____
_____
_____
_____
_____
_____
_____
_____

_____ ,

_____

Write a letter to the person you like (or hate) most in the world.
Use pictures instead of words wherever possible.

These people can't decide which hats to buy. Can you help them make up their minds?

Space explorers have discovered flowers growing on the
moons of Jupiter. What do they look like?

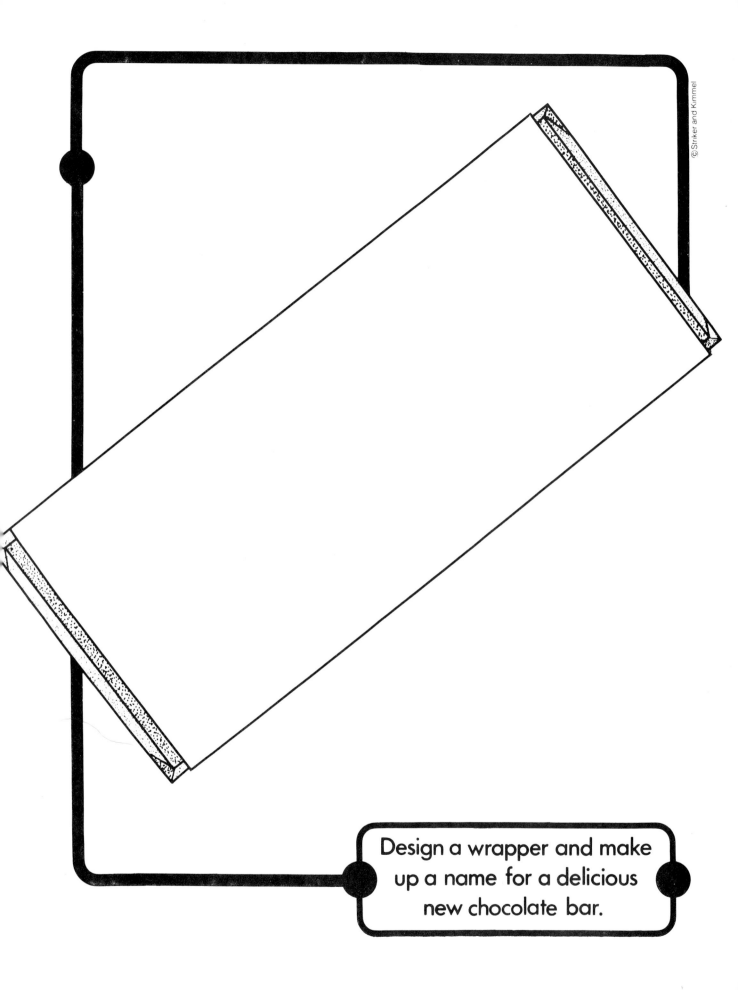

Design a wrapper and make up a name for a delicious new chocolate bar.

**What kinds of transportation
will we have in the year 2001?**

What do people do with their faces to show
how they are feeling?

This artist is about to paint a very strange picture. What will it look like?

STAR LIGHT, STAR BRIGHT
FIRST STAR I SEE TONIGHT

What do you wish for?

© Striker and Kimmel

I WISH I MAY
I WISH I MIGHT
HAVE THE WISH
I WISH TONIGHT

Where are these birds flying to?

ow do you look when you first get up in the morning?

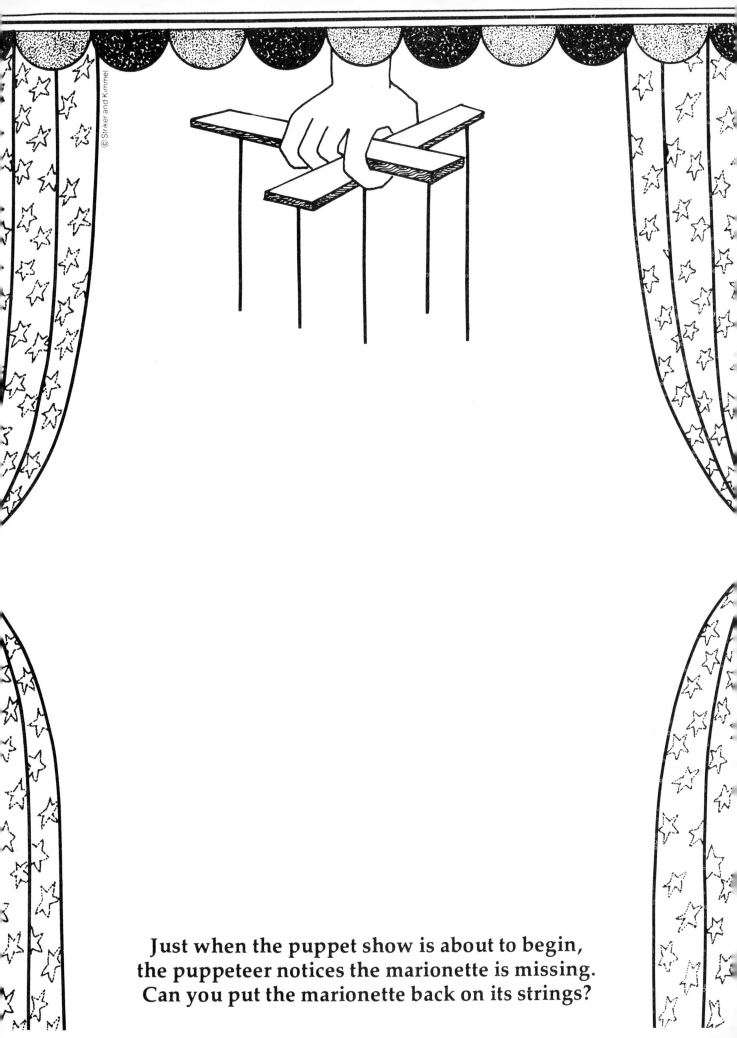

Just when the puppet show is about to begin,
the puppeteer notices the marionette is missing.
Can you put the marionette back on its strings?

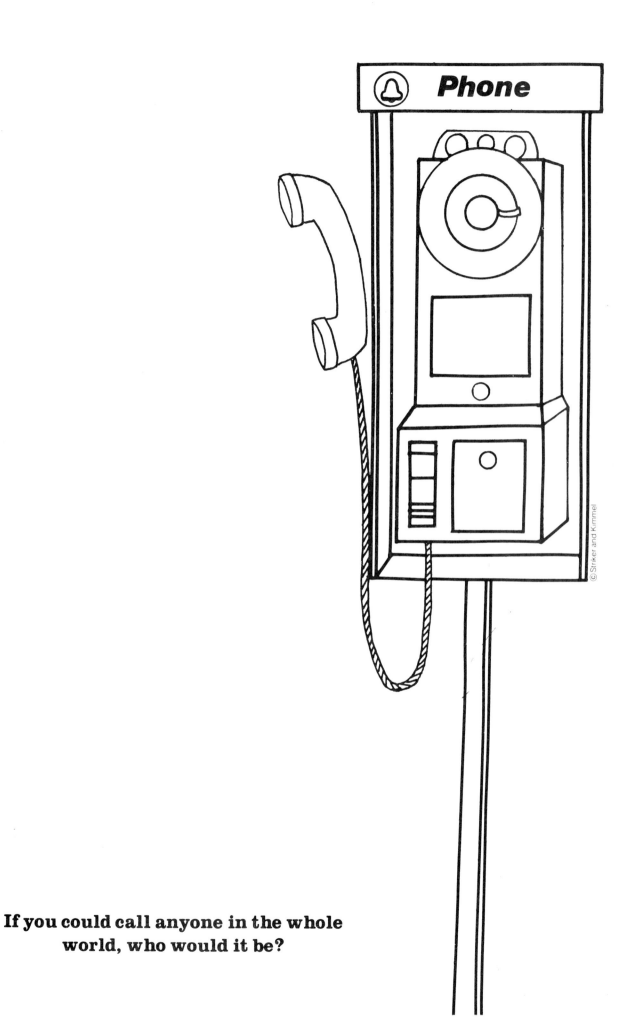

If you could call anyone in the whole world, who would it be?

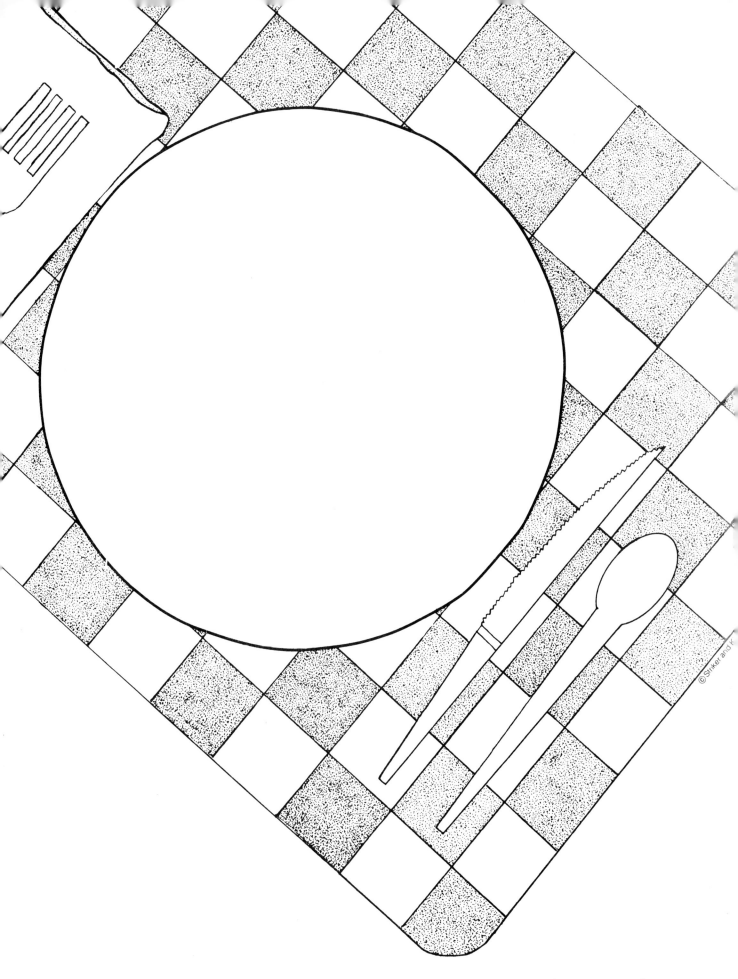

Design your own special dinner plate, to be used by you alone.

Dog Diner

Felix

Cat Care

Oops! We spilled ink on the last page of this book. Can you turn it into a picture?